VOLCANOES

ANN WEIL

SADDLEBACK
EDUCATIONAL PUBLISHING

DISASTERS

Air Disasters	Mountain Disasters
Deadly Storms	Sea Disasters
Earthquakes	Space Disasters
Ecological Disasters	Terrorism
Fire Disasters	**Volcanoes**

SADDLEBACK
EDUCATIONAL PUBLISHING
www.sdlback.com

ISBN-13: 978-1-61651-937-7
ISBN-10: 1-61651-937-1
eBook: 978-1-61247-633-9

Printed in Guangzhou, China
0000/CA00000000

17 16 15 14 13   1 2 3 4 5

Photo Credits: cover, pages 44, 45, USGS/Cascades Volcano Observatory; page 13, Bettmann/Corbis; page 30, Hulton-Deutsch Collection; page 53, Roger Ressmyer; page 65, © Johann Helgason | Dreamstime.com; page 74, © Marco Regalia | Dreamstime.com; page 85, © Jeff Grabert | Dreamstime.com

CONTENTS

DATAFILE

Timeline

August 28, 1963

Civil rights activist Martin Luther King Jr. gives his famous speech, "I Have a Dream."

November 8, 1963

An underwater volcano begins to erupt near Iceland. Later, it becomes the island Surtsey.

Where is Iceland?

HERE

Key Terms

magma—melted rock inside the earth

Ring of Fire—imaginary line that shows where tectonic plates meet

volcanologist—a scientist who studies volcanoes

CHAPTER 1 | Introduction

A mountain explodes. Big rocks are thrown high up into the sky. Burning hot lava rushes down the sides of the volcano. If there is a town or village nearby, this can mean disaster.

Erupting volcanoes kill many people. They also cause a lot of damage. But volcanoes aren't always bad news. Many people like to look at volcanoes. They travel long distances to see them. Vegetables grow better in soil near volcanoes. That means more food for the people who live there. Volcanoes produce some very beautiful gems and crystals. And the ash left in the air makes sunsets prettier.

There are volcanoes all over the world. There are even volcanoes in outer space! Most of Earth's volcanoes are underwater. But it's the volcanoes on land that cause the worst disasters.

What are Volcanoes?

Some volcanoes look like mountains. They are wide at the bottom and narrow on top. These are called cone volcanoes. They look like an upside-down ice cream cone. Some volcanoes don't look like mountains at all. They look like big holes in the ground.

Volcanoes are very different from mountains. They have a hollow center. It's like a big, long pipe that goes deep underground—all the way down through the Earth's crust.

The crust is the cool, hard surface of our planet. Earth may seem solid, but it's not. The Earth's crust is like a broken eggshell. Most volcanoes are along the cracks in the Earth's crust.

It is very, very hot inside our planet. It is so hot that rocks melt into liquid metal called magma. The huge pieces of the Earth's crust are called plates. Plates float on top of the magma. Magma can burst through the gaps between plates. This is how volcanoes are born.

Some volcanoes erupt frequently. These are called active volcanoes. Many volcanoes have not erupted for hundreds of years. These volcanoes are dormant, or "sleeping." Some volcanoes are considered extinct. This means we think they will never erupt again.

The Ring of Fire

Most active volcanoes are on the "Ring of Fire." The Ring of Fire is an imaginary line where plates meet.

And not all eruptions are violent. Some active volcanoes just let off steam. Only violent eruptions cause disasters. And there are usually warning signs before a volcano erupts with enough force to cause a disaster.

Warning Signs

People cannot stop a volcano from erupting. But there is still a lot we can do to avoid future volcano disasters.

Scientists who study volcanoes are called volcanologists. There are volcanologists all over the world. They work together to learn more about when and why volcanoes erupt. Volcanologists watch many active volcanoes. They are looking for signs that a volcano is about to erupt. Many disasters were avoided because people were evacuated before a volcano near them erupted.

Earthquakes are the most common warning sign. If there is an earthquake underneath a volcano, chances are that volcano is about to blow. Volcanoes and earthquakes often occur together where two plates meet. Both can result from shifts in the Earth's crust.

Earthquakes aren't the only warning sign. Magma rising up inside a volcano can make a lot of noise. Occasionally, the whole mountainside bulges from the force of the magma. Sometimes steam and gas come out of a volcano before it erupts. And there are usually small eruptions before a big one. All these warning signs give people a chance to escape.

But some volcanoes give no warning at all. These can be the deadliest volcano disasters of all.

A World of Volcanoes

Our planet was shaped by volcanoes. Millions of years ago, volcanoes covered the Earth. Eruptions created the land we live on today.

Japan

The islands of Japan are located on the Ring of Fire. The Japanese experience many earthquakes and volcanic eruptions.

Iceland

Iceland is made up of volcanic rock. Two plates underneath Iceland are pulling apart. This creates a crack in the Earth's crust. Magma flows out from this crack at the bottom of the ocean. It rises up and hardens into rock. This is how the island of Iceland was formed.

Underwater volcanoes continue to make new islands. An eruption near Iceland created Surtsey in 1963. The hot magma turns sea water into steam.

DATAFILE

Timeline

79 CE

Mount Vesuvius erupts in Pompeii. The entire city is buried under ash.

1631

Mount Vesuvius erupts again, killing more than 3,000 people.

Where is Pompeii?

Key Terms

CE—Common Era

Pompeii—an ancient Roman city in southern Italy

St. Elmo's Fire—sparks that look like lightning in the sky during a volcanic eruption

suffocate—to be unable to breathe oxygen

CHAPTER 2 | Mount Vesuvius, 79 CE

What's your worst nightmare? For some people it's being buried alive. But how about being buried alive under tons of burning ash? This happened to thousands of people when a volcano in southern Italy erupted in 79 CE.

Pompeii

Pompeii was an ancient Roman city. The people who lived there enjoyed a good life. Crops grew easily in the rich volcanic soil. There was plenty to eat. The city was built at the mouth of a river. It was a sea port on the Bay of Naples. Pompeii was a wealthy and beautiful city. And it was about to be buried under hot ash and volcanic rock.

Buried Alive

Mount Vesuvius erupted on a summer day in 79 CE. No one suspected that Mount Vesuvius was about to explode. Mount Vesuvius had not erupted for 800 years.

The citizens of Pompeii were going about their everyday lives. Some were home baking bread. Others were walking around town. Trades people were conducting business. Children played outside.

Suddenly, there was a big explosion. Huge rocks and burning ash rained down on Pompeii. In minutes, the hot ash was knee-deep. Clouds of poisonous gases covered the city. People suffocated. Their bodies lay where they fell. Soon the entire city was buried. No one was left alive.

The eruption also changed the landscape. The river no longer flowed there. The sea fell back away from where the city had been. Pompeii was gone. Before long, it was forgotten.

Ash and rock from Mount Vesuvius came down on other Roman cities. The town of Herculaneum was buried. But many people who lived there had time to escape. Other towns were also destroyed by the eruption. Survivors left the area.

Pompeii was rediscovered more than 1,500 years later. In the 1700s, people began to dig up Pompeii. They were amazed by what they found. The lava had hardened around the dead bodies. The bodies had rotted away. But the shapes of the people remained in the rock.

Food and buildings were also preserved. It was like finding a museum of daily life in ancient Rome.

Many tourists visit Pompeii. They see casts of people who were buried alive. It is fascinating, but also sad. It's too easy to imagine what their last moments were like.

Still Active

Mount Vesuvius has erupted many times since 79 CE. Most of these were minor. No one was hurt. But several were more serious. An eruption in 1631 killed more than 3,000 people. In 1794, a powerful eruption destroyed the town of Torre del Greco. A violent eruption in April 1906 lasted ten days. Two thousand people were killed. Many more thousands lost their homes. The volcano left places in ruin. Since then smaller eruptions have occurred in 1913, 1926, 1929, and 1944.

Mount Vesuvius is still active. It is the only active volcano on the mainland of Europe. More than two million people live near Mount Vesuvius now. If the volcano erupted today, they would all be in danger.

St. Elmo's Fire

People often see lightning during an eruption. But it's not a thunderstorm. The lightning is caused by static electricity. Sparks fly as tons of matter collide. This is called St. Elmo's Fire.

DATAFILE

Timeline

August 27, 1883

A volcano explodes the island of Krakatoa.

1927

The people who live on Krakatoa leave. It looks like the volcano may erupt again.

Where is Krakatoa?

HERE

Key Terms

Dutch East Indies—islands in the Indian Ocean now called Indonesia

steam pressure—a force created when water is heated to its boiling point

tsunami—a giant wave caused by a volcano or earthquake underwater

CHAPTER 3 | Krakatoa, 1883

Imagine a blast more powerful than the first atomic bomb. Imagine this explosion blowing up an entire island. This is what happened to Krakatoa in 1883. The planet shook when Krakatoa exploded. It was one of the greatest volcano disasters in recorded history.

Before the Big Blast

Krakatoa was a small island between Java and Sumatra. Java and Sumatra are also islands. Now these islands are part of Indonesia. But in the 1800s they were known as the Dutch East Indies.

No one was living on Krakatoa in 1883. Krakatoa was too small to attract settlers. It was in the middle of the Sunda Strait. Many trading ships sailed by Krakatoa. Most were traveling between the Indian Ocean and the China seas.

Pirates used the island as a base. They robbed the trade ships. Then they hid on Krakatoa. A small prison was built there in 1809. But it was abandoned long before the eruption.

Millions of people were living on Java and Sumatra in 1883. The coasts of both islands had many farming villages. The people who lived in these villages could see Krakatoa, which was about 25 miles away. It was about six miles long and two miles wide. Three volcano cones joined together into one big volcano.

Krakatoa's volcanoes had been dormant for generations. The Dutch officials had examined the burned-out craters. They thought the volcanoes were extinct.

There were warning signs that Krakatoa's volcanoes had become active. There were eruptions months before the big blast. A Dutchman visited the island to see what was going on. He reported back that there was a thick layer of ash over the island. He also saw steam rising from one of the craters.

Soon after, a huge black cloud hung over Krakatoa. Explosions continued. People couldn't sleep at night. There was too much noise. Most people were not frightened. Many other islands near them had volcanoes. They were used to volcanoes erupting. They expected Krakatoa to quiet down. But the opposite was about to happen.

The Big Bang

No one realized what was really happening. The first smaller eruptions had opened the middle of the volcano to the sea. Water was seeping inside. The hot magma turned the water into steam. The pressure inside increased. There was a huge build-up of steam pressure. Finally, the pressure was too great. It blew the mountain to pieces. The island of Krakatoa exploded on August 27, 1883. Red-hot rocks as big as a house were thrown high into the sky. Some of them went very far.

More than a thousand people on Java and Sumatra died immediately. Most of them were buried under burning rock and ash. It was one of the most violent explosions ever witnessed by human beings. It produced one of the loudest noises in history. People almost 3,000 miles away heard Krakatoa blow up.

It was such a powerful explosion that the volcano collapsed into the sea. Water rushed into the space where the volcano had been. Then the water rushed out again. This produced huge ocean waves called tsunami. Some were 100 feet high. That's taller than a ten-story building!

These huge waves smashed into the villages. About 34,000 people along the coasts of Java and Sumatra drowned. The waves also destroyed homes and property. This all happened in about half an hour. Hot ash from the volcano traveled more than 25 miles across the surface of the sea. More than 2,000 people were burned to death.

The Aftermath

The next day most of Krakatoa was gone. Pieces of the island were floating in the Indian Ocean. The wind blew bits of dust and ash everywhere.

People all over the world saw unusually colorful sunrises and sunsets for three years.

For days after the eruption, the sky was black with ash. It was as dark as night even in the daytime. But this didn't last forever. Plant life returned to the island. Coconuts floated to what was left of Krakatoa. They grew into trees. The wind and birds carried seeds there. These grew into plants. Within 14 years of the eruption, the island fragments had been colonized by at least 132 species of birds and insects. There were also 61 different plant species.

Some people started living on Krakatoa. In 1927, it looked like the volcano was going to erupt again. Everyone left the island. No one lives there anymore.

Krakatoa erupting

Tsunami

More people near Krakatoa died from tsunamis than during the actual eruption.

Underwater earthquakes and volcanoes can cause a tsunami. Out in the ocean, tsunamis travel faster than a speeding bullet. Near land, they suck up all the water near shore. Then they crash down. The wall of water smashes buildings. People are crushed and swept out to sea.

The word tsunami comes from Japan. It means "harbor wave."

DATAFILE

Timeline

April 1902

Mt. Pelée starts steaming on the island of
Martinique.

May 8, 1902

Mt. Pelée erupts. A stopped clock tells the time of
the eruption: 7:52 a.m.

Where is Martinique?

Did You Know?

One Mt. Pelée survivor was in jail when the volcano erupted. The thick walls of his cell protected him from the hot ash. The tiny window faced away from the mountain so poisonous gases didn't get in.

Key Terms

avalanche—a huge amount of rocks or snow falling down a mountain

boulder—a large, often round rock

crater—a hollow, bowl-shaped space

CHAPTER 4 | Mt. Pelée, 1902

In 1902, an entire city ignored a volcano's warning signs. Almost 30,000 people paid for that mistake with their lives. Mt. Pelée caused the most deaths from a single volcanic eruption during the 20th century.

St. Pierre was a city on the Caribbean island of Martinique. The city was completely destroyed when Mt. Pelée erupted in 1902. Only two people in the whole city survived!

Before the Blast

Mt. Pelée started steaming the first week of April 1902. This was about a month before the violent eruption. About two weeks later, an earthquake shook St. Pierre. Now we know that an earthquake near a volcano means trouble. But a hundred years ago, people didn't understand how volcanoes worked. The people of St. Pierre didn't make the connection between the earthquake and the volcano.

There were many small eruptions from the volcano. More and more ash floated down onto the city. These eruptions continued for about a week. Smelly gases from the volcano drifted down to the city. The odor was strong enough for people to notice. But the officials of St. Pierre were not alarmed. They didn't warn the residents.

If the same thing happened today, scientists would advise the authorities. People would be evacuated. But there were no volcano scientists in Martinique a hundred years ago.

On May 7th, a thunderous roar startled the people of St. Pierre. Two craters near the top of Mt. Pelée were glowing. There was a big cloud over the volcano. They could see flashes of lightning. Still, the city didn't empty out.

Then, on the morning of May 8, 1902, Mt. Pelée erupted. Deadly gas and burning ash rolled down the mountain. Now, it was too late to escape.

A Glowing Avalanche

Volcanic eruptions are not all alike. Sometimes there's a huge explosion that blows boulders into the air. Sometimes there's a lot of lava. Sometimes there's more ash and gases. When Mt. Pelée erupted in 1902, an enormous black cloud went straight up into the air. Another cloud of red-hot gases, ash, and stone rolled down the mountain. It looked like a glowing avalanche.

This glowing avalanche smothered the people of St. Pierre. No one could breathe. Within minutes, they suffocated. The ash burned their bodies. Buildings caught fire. Everything burned to the ground. When it was over, the city was gone. Only a few stone walls were left standing. A stopped clock recorded the exact time of the disaster. It happened at eight minutes to eight o'clock in the morning.

DATAFILE

Timeline

May 18, 1980

Mount St. Helens erupts. People hundreds of miles away can hear it.

November 4, 1980

Ronald Reagan is elected as the 40th president of the United States.

Where is Mount St. Helens?

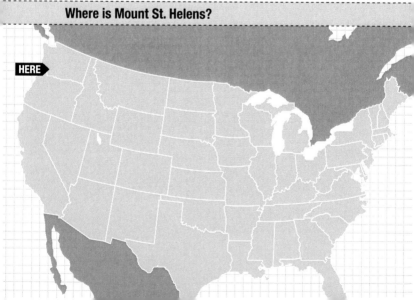

HERE

Key Terms

emergency zone—an area which may be dangerous

landslide—the swift movement of huge amounts of rocks and dirt down a hill

rubble—broken pieces of rock, brick, or building

CHAPTER 5 | Mount St. Helens, 1980

In 1980, a terrifying explosion blew the top off of Mount St. Helens in Washington state. Thousands of people might have been killed. Fortunately there were warning signs. People had time to leave their homes. Only 57 people died. But houses were ruined. Trees were reduced to piles of matchsticks. Lakes were filled with mud and rubble. Many wild animals died. And the landscape was changed forever.

Wake-Up Call

Mount St. Helens had last erupted in 1857. Then it was quiet for more than 120 years. But volcanologists were watching Mount St. Helens. Small earthquakes shook the mountain between 1975 and 1980. They expected an eruption. But they weren't sure exactly when.

At the beginning of 1980, the earthquakes became more powerful. They also happened more frequently. Next, there were small volcanic eruptions. This was two months before the big blast on May 18, 1980. The area around the volcano was declared an emergency zone. People packed everything they could. Then they sadly left their homes for the last time.

"...part of that mountain..."

Everyone had been warned. Most people had left the area by the beginning of May. But one elderly man wouldn't leave. His house was in the danger zone. A powerful earthquake shook his home. That was a week before the massive eruption that would kill him. The police tried to convince him to escape before it was too late. But he refused to go. He told them he was a "part of that mountain." He died when his house was buried under ash and stone.

Earthquakes, Landslide, a Volcano Erupts

Magma was collecting inside Mount St. Helens. More and more magma pushed up. This created a lot of pressure inside the volcano. The side of the mountain bulged.

On May 18, 1980, there was a powerful earthquake. It caused a landslide. The top of the mountain tumbled down. This triggered the eruption.

At first there was a big blast. Enormous rocks were thrown into the air. Ash and gas shot up 15 miles high. A huge ash cloud filled the sky. Lava poured down the side of the mountain. The eruption lasted nine hours. People hundreds of miles away could hear it. Then finally, it was all over.

Signs of Life Return

The eruption left the land looking like the surface of the moon. Still, land recovers quickly. Soon animals returned. Wild flowers pushed up through the ash. People used to come to the area to see the forest. They enjoyed visiting the park. Now tourists come to see the site of the eruption. It will take many years for trees to grow tall again. Till then, they can marvel at the effects of a volcano.

Mount St. Helens was 9,677 ft. (top photo), now it is 8,363 ft high. (bottom photo)

Mount Rainier is the highest peak in Washington state at 14,410 ft.

DATAFILE

Timeline

January 16, 1991

The Gulf War begins.

June 12, 1991

A dormant volcano, Mount Pinatubo, erupts in the Philippines.

Where are the Philippines?

Key Terms

caldera—a huge crater formed when a volcano collapses in on itself

lahar—mud which flows faster and farther than lava

seismograph—a machine which measures the strength of earthquakes

CHAPTER 6 | Mount Pinatubo

Mount Pinatubo was a dormant volcano. Then it erupted violently in 1991. This was one of the largest eruptions of the 20th century. Fortunately, there were early warning signs. Thousands of people were evacuated.

Their homes were destroyed. Their fields and crops were ruined. It was a major disaster for the Philippines. It also affected the rest of the world. Volcanic ash from the eruption circled the globe. It affected Earth's weather. It also produced spectacular sunsets.

Before the Blast

The first hint of trouble occurred mid-March 1991. Earthquakes shook villages on the lower slopes of Mount Pinatubo. Over the next weeks, there were more earthquakes. Then gas and steam started to rise from the volcano.

Volcano science has come a long way in the past hundred years. Now, people take notice whenever a volcano shows signs of activity. We have learned from Mt. Pelée and other volcanoes.

Scientists installed seismographs to measure the earthquakes. They knew the volcano was no longer dormant. But would it erupt violently? Many lives depended on the answer.

The scientists gathered data. It all pointed to a huge eruption. And they were quite sure it would happen very soon. They recommended that people leave the area.

More than 30,000 people lived on the slopes of the volcano. Many more Filipinos lived on the flat land surrounding the volcano.

Americans and their families were also in the area. They lived on two military bases not far from the volcano. Clark Air Base was about 15 miles away. Subic Bay Naval Station was about 25 miles away.

Everyone was evacuated. But the eruption still affected hundreds of thousands of Filipinos.

Before the eruption, Filipino farmers benefited from the fertile volcanic soil, a gift from ancient Mount Pinatubo. Eruptions thousands of years ago had enriched the soil with volcanic minerals. Now Pinatubo was about to cover these fields with so much ash that they would become unusable.

1991 Eruption

The first large eruption occurred on June 12, 1991. The volcano exploded upwards with tremendous force. The eruptions that followed over the next two days were even more powerful.

On June 15th the top of the volcano collapsed. It left a huge crater more than a mile wide.

A big cloud of ash rose into the sky. The sun was blocked out for many days. It was as dark as night even in the middle of the day. Gas and ash from Mount Pinatubo spread all around the world. A lot of ash fell to the ground near the volcano. It smothered the land with a thick coating of dust.

Mud, Mud, and More Mud

The eruption of Mount Pinatubo was devastating. But worse damage was still to come. By unlucky chance, a very wet tropical storm hit the area just after the eruption. It rained down on Mount Pinatubo. The water turned tons of volcanic ash to mud.

Mudflows, called lahars, raced down the sides of the volcano. They went faster and farther than the lava. Lahars took out bridges. Mud flooded homes and fields. It was as if millions of loads of concrete had been spread over the entire region.

Hundreds of people died. Many families lost their homes and their farms. There wasn't as much food. There was no grass for farm animals to graze. It took many years for people to recover.

Mount Pinatubo's caldera

Caldera

Sometimes a volcano collapses after a very violent explosion. This happens because all the magma rushes out at once. Then the empty volcano falls in on itself. This creates a huge crater called a caldera.

DATAFILE

Timeline

January 3, 1983

Hawaiian volcano Kilauea starts erupting. It is still erupting today.

March 25, 1984

Hawaiian volcano Mauna Loa's last eruption begins.

Where is Hawaii?

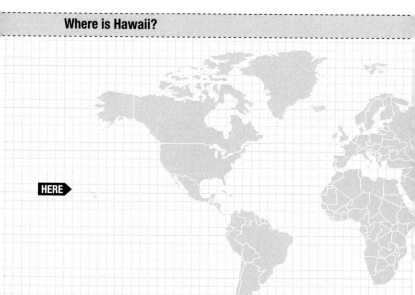

HERE

Key Terms

shield volcano—a volcano which slopes gently upward and looks like a shield

tourism—the business of bringing travelers to a place for pleasure

CHAPTER 7 | Hawaii's Gentle Giants

The Hawaiian islands were formed by underwater volcanoes. Some of these volcanoes are now extinct. Others are active. Mauna Loa last erupted in 1984. Kilauea has been erupting nonstop since 1983.

Hawaiian volcanoes don't explode like the ones that destroyed Pompeii and St. Pierre. There's no big bang! Instead, they produce a lot of lava. The lava flows out of the volcano and spreads across the land. It flows over roads and destroys homes and property.

There are benefits along with the risks. The Hawaiian volcanoes are a tourist attraction. Many people travel to Hawaii to see them. Tourism provides a source of income for many Hawaiians.

Another advantage is the rich volcanic soil. Lots of fruits and other crops grow well there. Hawaii is famous for its pineapples. Many Hawaiians depend on the land for food. They also sell fruits and other produce to make money.

But living with active volcanoes is risky, even when the eruptions are not violent. Volcanoes are often unpredictable. No one knows in advance how much lava will be produced during each eruption. Disaster may not be far away.

Mauna Loa

Mauna Loa is the world's biggest volcano. It is much larger than the cone-shaped volcanoes that occur along the Ring of Fire. Mauna Loa is a shield volcano. Shield volcanoes slope gently upward. They do not form cones. Mauna Loa is shaped like a mound or shield, like the shields used by ancient warriors.

Mauna Loa is a very active volcano. It has erupted 33 times since 1843. Now people keep track of when volcanoes erupt. But there is nothing written about Mauna Loa's eruptions before 1843. Scientists think the first eruption of Mauna Loa occurred about a million years ago. Since then there have been many eruptions. The lava from these eruptions created the enormous mound that is Mauna Loa today.

1950 Eruption

There had been an eruption a year earlier, in 1949. But it was not so spectacular as the one that began June 1, 1950. This was the largest recorded eruption. This eruption lasted 23 days. It erupted 376 million cubic meters of lava (492 yards). Lava flowed from a 12-mile-long (20 km) crack in the volcano. Fountains of lava shot up as high as 50 m (164 feet). One lava flow traveled 15 miles in less than three hours. It was slow enough for people to escape. But the lava destroyed a gas station and post office. Many homes were destroyed. Lava also destroyed a coconut grove.

Different parts of the volcano were erupting at the same time. There were many different lava flows. Some people wanted to see the lava. They gathered along a highway waiting for it to appear. But police told them to move. A plane had flown over the area. They were watching the lava from the air. The lava was coming too close to the highway. If the people had stayed, they would have been trapped and died.

Kilauea

Kilauea is one of the world's most active volcanoes. It's right next to Mauna Loa on the Island of Hawaii. Its first recorded eruption occurred in 1790. It has been very active ever since. Some of these eruptions lasted only a short time. Others went on for months, even years. The rate of eruptions has increased since 1924. Now it erupts continuously.

Kilauea has been erupting nonstop for about 20 years. By 2002 it had produced about 2.3 cubic km (81,224 cubic feet) of lava. This lava has spread over 110 sq km (42.5 square miles). It has destroyed hundreds of homes. A national park visitor's center and a 700-year-old Hawaiian temple were also destroyed. Sometimes lava flows over roads and highways. They must be repaired before cars can drive over them. Some of this lava flows into the sea. This produces huge steam clouds. It also makes the island bigger.

Lava continues to flow from Kilauea. There is no sign that it is slowing down.

Scientists Can Save Lives

Scientists study the Hawaiian volcanoes. They can't prevent volcanoes from erupting. But their work can save lives. Volcanoes are unpredictable. But the more we know about them, the better we can avoid future disasters.

DATAFILE

Timeline

January 2, 2010

In the African country of the Democratic Republic of the Congo, the Nyamuragira volcano erupts.

November 7, 2011

Nyamuragira, the highly active volcano in the Democratic Republic of the Congo, erupts with lava flowing from a new fissure.

Where is the DR of the Congo?

Key Terms

channel—a trench, furrow, or groove

fissure—a long, narrow opening or line of breakage made by cracking or splitting, especially in rock or earth

geyser—a hot spring in which water intermittently boils, sending a tall column of water and steam into the air

torch—to set on fire

CHAPTER 8 | The World's Most Active Volcanoes

Volcanoes are found all over the Earth's surface. They start out as fissures in the Earth's crust. When volcanoes erupt, lava (melted rock), ash, steam, and other gases shoot out. Over time, the lava and ash build up to form a mountain. Volcanoes can be as big as other kinds of mountains. There are even volcanoes underneath the ocean floor.

Volcanic eruptions can be like bombs going off. There is hot liquid rock under the surface of a volcano. This is called magma. Pressure inside the mountain builds up. Then magma blasts out of the mountain. It is now called lava. Hot lava moves very fast, up to 60 miles per hour. Lava usually destroys anything in its path.

When a volcano erupts, it can affect the entire world. In 2010, Iceland's Eyjafjallajokull volcano erupted. Huge clouds of rocky ash exploded into the air. The power of the blast shot the ash high into

Mount Eyjafjallajokul in Iceland is 5,466 feet tall.

the Earth's atmosphere. The ash clouds closed air travel all over Europe for almost a week.

Volcanoes are usually classified as active, dormant, or extinct. An active volcano is one that has erupted recently. In volcano terms, "recently" means within the last few thousand years. Scientists believe active volcanoes will erupt again.

Nyamuragira Volcano, Democratic Republic of the Congo

The Nyamuragira Volcano is located in the Virunga National Park in the Democratic Republic of the Congo. It is over 10,000 feet high.

Since 1885, Nyamuragira has erupted over 30 times. There have been two recent eruptions at Nyamuragira. The first, in January 2010, sprayed lava down its southern face. Local residents south of the volcano rushed outside to see lava flowing toward their villages. The lava torched plants and shrubs as it swept down. The villagers were far enough away to escape harm.

The Nyamuragira volcano erupted again in 2012. Huge geysers of liquid lava burst through a crack in the mountain's peak. The crack was more than a half-mile wide. Chunks of lava shot almost 2,000 feet in the air. Some residents were evacuated. Some parts of the mountainside caught fire. But there were no injuries.

Scientists monitoring the Nyamuragira volcano reported a series of tremors just before the 2012 eruption. Strong vibrations from the Nyamuragira eruption could trigger an eruption of the nearby Nyiragongo volcano. If this happened, lava could flow into the major city of Goma, which is just 25 miles away from Nyiragongo. This could be disastrous for residents. The temperature of lava can reach 2,000 degrees Fahrenheit!

Mount Etna, Italy

Mount Etna is located on the east coast of Sicily. Etna is Italy's most active volcano. It is also the tallest at nearly 11,000 feet. Mount Etna has been erupting regularly for thousands of years. In 2011, more than 15 eruptions were recorded on Mount Etna.

On January 11, 2011, scientists recorded several tremors around Mount Etna. The next day, the volcano erupted. Lava and ash blew out from the top of the mountain. Large rocks called "lava bombs" bounced down the face of the mountain. Lava spewed for almost 45 minutes. Spider webs of bright orange lava ran down the mountain.

A year later, Mount Etna erupted again. The mountain shot out red-hot lava blasts that splattered on the snow-covered mountain. The eruption lasted several hours. The glow from the lava was so bright it lit up villages like it was daytime. A blanket of black ash settled on the white snow at the upper reaches of the mountain.

Mount Stromboli, Italy

The island of Stromboli sits at the northeast tip of the Aeolian Islands off the west coast of southern Italy. At its peak, the mountain is only about 3,000 feet above sea level. Mount Stromboli is a tourist attraction called the "Lighthouse of the

Mediterranean." Tour groups arrive daily to visit the island and watch the volcano erupt.

Mount Stromboli has been erupting regularly for more than 2,000 years! Luckily, most of these eruptions create minor steam clouds and small bubbling pools of lava.

In April 2009, there was a large eruption at Mount Stromboli. Big clouds of toxic ash had been floating around the summit for days. Residents reported hearing hissing sounds. The hissing got louder. There was an explosion of ash and orange lava. It lasted a few seconds. Then the mountain went silent. Thicker clouds of steam rose above the peak. Then, there was another, larger explosion of lava. The sky lit up in bright fireworks of stone, lava, and ash.

The lava flowed down a channel of rock toward the sea. The lava reached the sea as a flowing orange river. It hit the water and exploded in thick clouds of steam. Then the lava hardened into gray blobs.

DATAFILE

Timeline

December 18, 2000

The Popocatepetl volcano near Mexico City, Mexico, erupts sending red-hot rocks, smoke, and ash 2.5 miles into the air.

April 25, 2012

About 40 miles southeast of Mexico City, the Popocatepetl volcano erupts with smoke and ash.

Where is Mexico?

Key Terms

catastrophic—extremely harmful; bringing physical or financial ruin

molten—liquified by heat

seismic waves—vibration produced by an earthquake

summit—the highest point of a hill or mountain

Volcanoes located near densely populated areas are especially dangerous. When dangerous volcanoes erupt near cities or villages, many people can die. Local residents are exposed to dangerous risks. These include large falling rocks, landslides, tsunamis, and hot lava flows.

Popocatepetl Volcano, Mexico City

Mexico City has a population of nearly 9 million people. If you include surrounding areas, it is more like 20 million. Mexico City is just 40 miles east of the nearly 18,000-foot-high Popocatepetl ("Popo") volcano.

In April of 2012, Popocatepetl erupted. Nearby villagers described hearing a low rumbling sound. The ground shook. Tall plumes of ash and smoke exploded into the sky. Small but loud eruptions started. In two hours, there were twelve separate eruptions.

Molten rocks shot a half-mile into the air. Large mudslides roared down the sides of the mountain. The ash clouds even closed down the busy airport at Puebla. Police evacuated the village of Xalitzintla. This village was just seven miles from the volcano. More than 2,500 people lived there. Everyone survived.

Mount Merapi, Indonesia

Merapi means "mountain of fire" in Indonesian. The volcano is located in a densely populated area in central Java. Merapi has been erupting constantly since the 1500s. An eruption in 2006 killed more than 5,000 people and left 200,000 homeless.

The active and snowcapped Popocatepetl volcano in Mexico is over 17,800 feet.

On October 26, 2010, Mount Merapi erupted again. Geysers of mud, lava, and gas sent terrified residents running down the mountain. Dark ash fell like snow on the surrounding areas. The nearby Gendol River ran thick with mud, ash, and splintered trees. More than 30 people were killed.

Temporary shelters were set up for hundreds of people. A mass burial was held for dozens of victims. Then another major eruption hit. This was devastating because many residents had returned after escaping the first eruption.

Boiling hot gas escaped, and mud and rock rushed down the southern slope of Merapi at nearly 60 miles per hour. The temperature of the ash cloud that hit several villages was nearly 1,000 degrees Fahrenheit. The gases were so hot they burned villages more than nine miles away.

Medical workers handed out blankets, masks, and eyedrops. Doctors reported that many survivors had breathing problems from the thick dust and sand in the air. Many children suffered burning throats and eye infections.

More than 165 people were killed in the Merapi explosion. Over 90,000 people were left homeless.

Nevado del Ruiz Volcano, Colombia

Nevado del Ruiz is the highest volcano in Colombia. It is over 17,500 feet high. Even though it is close to the equator, the summit of the mountain is covered in snow.

On the night of November, 13 1985, Nevado del Ruiz exploded. Thick clouds of ash spit out of the mountain. The local Red Cross ordered an evacuation. But then the ash clouds stopped. The evacuation was called off.

Then, Nevado del Ruiz erupted again. Blasts of rock and lava blew out of the mountain. It melted the snow. The hot water picked up debris and rushed down the mountain. Large boulders bounced down the slopes. In surrounding villages, it was pitch black outside. All the electricity was out. Ash clouds blocked the moonlight. Villagers ran out onto the streets. Cars were floating in rushing waters. Rivers of mud bulldozed houses and buried people.

The town of Chinchina was destroyed. Nearly 2,000 people were killed. Another flow of lava and mud wiped out the town of Armero. Armero had been built on top of a previous lava and mud flow. Over 20,000 people were killed in Armero.

Mount Rainier, Washington State, USA

Mount Rainier looks beautiful and peaceful. But Mount Rainier is actually a dangerous volcano. It is over 14,000 feet high. Rainier is dangerous because it is located just 50 miles from the city of Seattle.

More than three million people live in areas around Mount Rainier. Many are living on old mudflows from previous eruptions hundreds or thousands of years ago. If Mount Rainier erupted, people living in these areas would have only minutes to escape. Huge rivers of lava and burning gas and rock might devastate many communities. The destruction might even reach downtown Seattle. The earthquake effects of the eruption could cause tsunamis in Puget Sound and Lake Washington.

Mount Fuji, Japan

The islands of Japan have more than 100 volcanoes. Each year at least one erupts. Mount Fuji has not erupted since 1707. But scientists consider it one of the most dangerous volcanoes in the world.

In 2000, volcano scientists (volcanologists) discovered something very scary. They had recorded several low-level earthquakes near Mount Fuji. The great mountain was shaking. This was a potentially catastrophic finding. The city of Tokyo is just 70 miles away from Mount Fuji. More than 30 million people live in Tokyo.

Scientists conducted a series of test explosions near the base of Mount Fuji. The explosions created seismic waves. Studying the waves, scientists learned that hot material called "magma" was building up deep inside the mountain. At some point, the pressure of the magma inside Mount Fuji might cause a full volcanic eruption. Scientists are keeping a close watch on this and other dangerous volcanoes.

DATAFILE

Timeline

July 29, 1968

Costa Rica's Arenal volcano unexpectedly erupts, with violent explosions lasting over three days.

August 2000

The top of Costa Rica's Arenal volcano explodes, sending rivers of hot ash and mud rushing down the mountainside and destroying trees and buildings in its path.

Where is Costa Rica?

HERE

Key Terms

composition—the nature of something's ingredients; what something is made of

lava bomb—mass of molten rock larger than 2.5 inches in diameter

lava dome—mounds of lava that collect around a volcanic vent

sandblasted—roughen or clean with a jet of sand

vibration—rapid quivers or trembles

CHAPTER 10 | Surprise Volcanic Eruptions

When will a volcano erupt? Predicting an eruption could potentially save thousands of lives. Scientists who study volcanoes, called volcanologists, look for clues. They study past eruptions. They use sophisticated equipment to detect changes in the air's composition around the volcano. And they monitor seismic activity for even the smallest vibration. The volcanologists at the US Geological Survey saved thousands of lives in 1980 when they convinced local officials that Mount St. Helens was going to erupt.

Chaitén Volcano, Southern Chile

Silent for thousands of years, Chaitén erupted on May 2, 2008. The explosion blasted gas and hot ash miles into the air over Chaitén, a small town located just 6 miles from the volcano. Chaitén was completely covered in gray ash.

Hot boulders and ash rolled down the mountain like an avalanche. Rivers of mud, ash, and rock poured into the Chaitén River Valley. Acres of forest burned to the ground. Thousands of residents evacuated. At least one person died.

Inside the Chaitén volcano, tons of boiling magma moved toward the summit. The pressure of the magma formed a "lava dome," which collapsed. Wide rivers of hot ash and debris shot down the valley toward Chaitén. Acres of farmland were destroyed. The government of Chile finally moved the town of Chaitén away from the volcano.

Arenal Volcano, Costa Rica

Arenal is a nearly 5,500-foot volcano located near Lake Arenal in northern Costa Rica. It is one of the most active volcanoes in Costa Rica. Arenal's last major eruption in 1968 killed nearly 90 people.

There have been several eruptions of Arenal over the last 35 years.

In August of 2000, scientists recorded a series of small tremors in the ground around Arenal. Clouds of ash and gas were rising over the crater of the mountain. Then the summit of Arenal exploded.

Geysers of hot ash and toxic gases shot out of the volcano. "Lava bombs" launched out of the mountain and landed more than three miles away. Huge rivers of ash, mud, and hot boulders moved down the mountain at great speed. Trees and buildings were destroyed.

A group of tourists were caught in a flow of searing ash and rock that reached speeds of 50 miles an hour. An eight-year-old American girl was killed along with a local guide. Several others survived, but with serious burns. The nearby Arenal National Park was evacuated.

The Arenal volcano in Costa Rica is 5,437 feet.

Unzen Volcano, Kyushu, Japan

Mount Unzen is on the Japanese island of Kyushu, about 25 miles east of the city of Nagasaki. In 1792, Mount Unzen erupted. One of Unzen's lava domes collapsed into the sea and triggered a tsunami that killed as many as 15,000 people.

In May of 1991, small rivers of lava seeped through the summit of Unzen. Clouds of smoke drifted over the mountain. Small pools of orange lava bubbled to the surface of the volcano. Many residents of the area were evacuated, But some residents chose to stay in their homes. They believed the volcano was not going to erupt.

On June 3, Unzen exploded. Rivers of hot ash, mud, and lava flowed at 50 miles per hour down the mountain. This flow killed 43 people. Some were volcano scientists. Some were journalists. And some were local residents.

The ash and rocks continued flowing down the mountain. They swept away bridges and roads. Rescue crews were blocked from getting in to help people. Many survivors were rescued by helicopter. Thousands of acres of farmland were destroyed.

By the end of the eruption cycle, more than 2,000 buildings had been destroyed.

Taal Volcano, The Philippines

Taal is a volcano located on the island of Luzon in the Philippines. It is located about 30 miles from the heavily populated capital, Manila. Taal is one of the most active volcanoes in the Philippines.

Taal's dozens of eruptions can be traced as far back to the 16th century, when Augustinian friars settled near the volcano. One of Taal's most devastating eruptions occurred in 1911. Steam and ash from the eruption killed over 1,000 people.

In 1965, an eruption created high-speed surges of ash, mud, and rocks. Villages around Lake Taal were "sandblasted" and drowned in the flow. Residents living close to the volcano were unable to escape. Approximately 200 people lost their lives.

Taal's last eruption was a minor one in 1977. In June of 2010, the Philippine Institute of Volcanology raised the threat level on Taal. This indicated that scientists believed the volcano could erupt at any time.

Nyiragongo Volcano, Democratic Republic of the Congo

Nyiragongo is one of the most active volcanoes in Africa. But in recent history, this volcano has struck with little warning. In 1977, a lake of lava that formed in the volcano cracked, sending streams of lava rushing down its sides. The lava lake drained in only an hour. The exact number of people killed will never be known.

On January 17, 2002, the Nyiragongo volcano erupted again. Fissures opened up on the sides of the mountain. Fissures even opened up in the middle of the city of Goma. Lava flowed out of the fissures. Rivers of lava streamed down the mountain. Fourteen villages near the Rwandan border were destroyed. Thousands were left homeless.

Many homeless people ran toward Goma to escape the lava. Clouds of ash were falling over Goma, which is just 30 miles from the volcano. The rivers of hot lava poured through the city of 400,000. Goma started to catch fire. Some of the lava flows were more than 300 feet wide. Nearly 40 percent of Goma was eventually covered in lava and mud.

Days after the eruption, desperate Congolese residents gathered fuel at a gas station. Hot lava from the Nyiragongo volcano ignited the gasoline. A giant orange fireball exploded into the air. More than 100 people were killed.

Glossary

avalanche—a huge amount of rocks or snow falling down a mountain

boulder—a large, often round rock

caldera—a huge crater formed when a volcano collapses in on itself

catastrophic—extremely harmful; bringing physical or financial ruin

CE—Common Era

channel—a trench, furrow, or groove

composition—the nature of something's ingredients; what something is made of

crater—a hollow, bowl-shaped space

Dutch East Indies—islands in the Indian Ocean now called Indonesia

emergency zone—an area which may be dangerous

fissure—a long, narrow opening or line of breakage made by cracking or splitting, especially in rock or earth

geyser—a hot spring in which water intermittently boils, sending a tall column of water and steam into the air

lahar—mud which flows faster and farther than lava

landslide—the swift movement of huge amounts of rocks and dirt down a hill

lava bomb—mass of molten rock larger than 2.5 inches in diameter

lava dome—mounds of lava that collect around a volcanic vent

molten—liquified by heat

Pompeii—an ancient Roman city in southern Italy

rubble—broken pieces of rock, brick, or building

sandblasted—roughen or clean with a jet of sand

seismic waves—vibration produced by an earthquake

seismograph—a machine which measures the strength of earthquakes

shield volcano—a volcano which slopes gently upward and looks like a shield

steam pressure—a force created when water is heated to its boiling point

St. Elmo's Fire—sparks that look like lightning in the sky during a volcanic eruption

suffocate—to be unable to breathe oxygen

summit—the highest point of a hill or mountain

torch—to set on fire

tourism—the business of bringing travelers to a place for pleasure

tsunami—a giant wave caused by a volcano or earthquake underwater

vibration—rapid quivers or trembles

volcanologist—a scientist who studies volcanoes

Index